Peruvian Cuisine

By Philip Martin McCaulay

Peruvian Cuisine

Published in Raleigh, North Carolina, USA
ISBN: 978-0-557-19543-5

Peruvian Cuisine

Appetizers and Salads	Anticucho (Beef Heart Stew)	8
	Causa	22
	Causa Rellena con Cangrejo (with Crab)	24
	Causa Rellena con Pollo (with Chicken)	28
	Ceviche de Pescado (Fish)	30
	Ceviche de Camarones y Pescado (Shrimp and Fish)	32
	Ensalada de Pallares (Lima Bean Salad)	42
	Ocopa (Peruvian Green Sauce)	48
	Ocopa de Camarones (Shrimp)	50
	Papas a la Huancaína (Potatoes)	52
	Pulpo al Olivo (Octopus in Olive Sauce)	60
	Tiradito (new cousin of Ceviche)	72
Entrees	Adobo de Chancho (Spicy Pork)	2
	Aji de Gallina (Peppered Hen)	4
	Arroz con Mariscos (Shellfish & Rice)	12
	Arroz con Pollo (Chicken and Rice)	14
	Arroz Tapado (Covered Rice)	18
	Bistec a lo Pobre (Poor Man's Steak)	20
	Chicharrón de Cerdo (Fried Pork)	36
	Choros a la Chalaca (Mussels)	38
	Chupe de Camarones (Shrimp Soup)	40
	Estofado de Pollo (Chicken Stew)	44
	Lomo Saltado (Jumping Beef)	46
	Papa Rellena (Stuffed Potato)	54
	Pescado a la Chorrillana (Fish)	56
	Rocoto Relleno (Stuffed Hot Peppers)	62
	Seco de Cordero (Lamb Stew)	66
	Tacu-Tacu	70
	Tortillas de Camarones (Shrimp)	74
Desserts	Alfajores (Peruvian Cookies)	6
	Arroz con Leche (Rice Pudding)	10
	Suspiro a la Limeña (Lima-Style Sigh)	68
Drinks	Chicha Morada (Purple Corn Drink)	30
	Pisco Sour	58

Table of Contents

Peruvian Cuisine

This book is a collection of the most popular authentic Peruvian recipes. Peruvian Cuisine is considered one of the most diverse in the world and is on par with French, Chinese and Indian cuisine. In January 2004, The Economist stated that "Peru can lay claim to one of the world's dozen or so great cuisines", while at the Fourth International Summit of Gastronomy Madrid Fusión 2006, regarded as the world's most important gastronomic forum, held in Spain between January 17 and 19, Lima was declared the "Gastronomic Capital of the Americas".

Thanks to its pre-Incas and Inca heritage and to Spanish, Basque, African, Sino-Cantonese, Japanese and finally Italian, French and British immigration (mainly throughout the 19th century), Peruvian cuisine combines the flavors of four continents. With the eclectic variety of traditional dishes, the Peruvian culinary arts are in constant evolution, and impossible to list in their entirety. Suffice it to mention that along the Peruvian coast alone there are more than two thousand different types of soups, and that there are more than 250 traditional desserts. The great variety in Peruvian cuisine stems from three major influences:

- Peru's unique geography
- Peru's openness and blending of distinct ethnicities and cultures
- The incorporation of ancient cuisine into modern Peruvian cuisine

1

Adobo de Chancho (Spicy Pork)

Ingredients

- 1 whole head garlic
- salt, freshly ground pepper
- 2 tablespoons lard or vegetable oil
- 2 tablespoons ground annatto (achiote)
- 1 cup white vinegar
- juice of 1 Seville (bitter) orange, or 1/4 cup orange juice
- 2 teaspoons ground cumin
- 3 pounds shoulder of pork, cut into 2-inch cubes
- 1-1/2 pounds sweet potatoes

Preparation

1. Peel the garlic cloves and reduce them to a puree in an electric blender with the annatto, cumin, salt and pepper to taste, and vinegar.
2. Put the pork pieces into a large bowl and pour the garlic marinade over them, mixing well. Marinate overnight in the refrigerator, covered. Strain, saving the marinade.
3. Pat the pork cubes dry with paper towels. Heat the lard or oil in a large skillet and sauté the pork pieces until golden brown all over, transferring them to a casserole as they are done.

4. Pour the marinade over the pork, add the orange juice, cover, and cook over very low heat until the meat is tender, 1-1/2 to 2 hours.

5. Peel the sweet potatoes and cut them into slices about 3/4 inch thick. Cook in boiling salted water until tender, 15 to 20 minutes. Drain.

6. To serve, heap the pork in the center of a large warmed platter and surround with the sweet potato slices moistened with a little of the meat gravy. White rice is another traditional accompaniment to this dish.

Aji de Gallina (Peppered Hen)

Ingredients

- 4 lb (1300g) chicken
- 1/2 cup (120ml) of olive oil
- ¼ lb (110g) of chopped pecans
- 3 hot yellow South American chilis (seeds removed) (Adjust quantity for individual taste)
- ¼ loaf of bread
- 1 can evaporated milk
- 4 oz (110g) grated Parmesan cheese.
- 1 large finely chopped onion
- 1 chicken bouillon cube
- Salt and pepper to taste
- 6 Potatoes
- 1/2 cup (120g) of black olives
- 4 hard boiled eggs
- Boiled rice; sufficient for 8 servings

Preparation

1. Boil chicken in salted water together with the bouillon cube. Remove bones and break into bite size pieces, keeping the resulting chicken stock.
2. In a saucepan, heat oil and sauté the onion, garlic, and finely chopped chili peppers and add salt and pepper. Fry this until the onions are cooked and golden.
3. Soak the bread in 2 cups of the stock from the boiled chicken and place in a blender for a

couple of minutes and then add the resulting liquid to the saucepan.

4. Cook slowly for 10 minutes. Cook slowly, stirring to thicken.
5. Add the chopped pecans, grated cheese, and chicken pieces. Cook until it has a thick creamy texture. About 5 minutes before serving add the evaporated milk and continue cooking on low heat.
6. Serve over the boiled rice and garnish with halved potatoes, eggs quartered lengthwise, and olives.

Makes 8 servings.

Alfajores (Peruvian Cookies)

Alfajores are a Latin-American dessert that melt in the mouth.

Ingredients

- 1/2 cup butter,
- 1 cup sugar,
- 1 egg,
- 2 egg yolks,
- 1 tsp. vanilla,
- 2 tsp. lemon rind, grated,
- 1 1/2 cup cornstarch,
- 1/2 cup flour,
- 1 tsp. baking powder, and
- 1/4 tsp. salt.

Preparation

1. Cream butter; add sugar and beat until fluffy.
2. Add egg and egg yolks, one at a time, beating well.
3. Beat in vanilla and lemon rind.
4. Sift together cornstarch, flour, baking powder and salt.
5. Add to mixture and mix well.
6. Drop batter by small spoonfuls onto well buttered baking sheet.
7. Bake at 350 degrees for 15 minutes.
8. Remove immediately. Sandwich the cookies together with (dulce de leche) sweet milk dessert. Caramel may be substituted.

Makes 40 cookies.

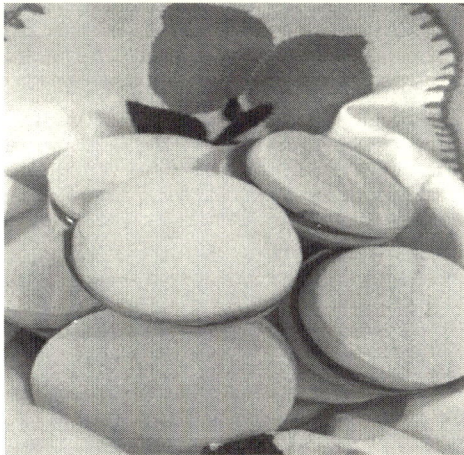

Anticucho (Beef Heart Stew)

Anticucho is one of the most popular dishes in Peru. It is often sold by street vendors and accompanied by corn-on-the-cob and portions of cold boiled potato with a spot of chili sauce. Those whose tastes do not extend to trying beef heart may substitute any good cut of red meat, though this is not the authentic Peruvian style.

Ingredients (for 5 people)

Anticucho accompanied by lettuce, potato and corn-on-the-cob

- 1 Beef heart
- 2 cloves of garlic
- ¼ of a cup ground spicy red chili
- 2 cups of brown vinegar
- 1 teaspoon of ground cumin
- 1 teaspoon of achiote (annatto)
- 1 teaspoon of salt
- 1 teaspoon of ground black pepper

Preparation

1. Place all the above ingredients, other than the heart, in a bowl and mix thoroughly.
2. Clean the heart, removing all fat. Cut into bite size cubes. Place the heart pieces into the marinade mixture and leave to marinate for about 10 hours or overnight. The heart should be completely covered.

3. After marinating, insert meat on skewers. At this stage if desired, some additional ingredients such as green pepper or red pepper (capsicum) or corn-on-cob (cut to a similar size to the heart, may be also inserted on the skewers.)

4. The skewered heart should then be cooked on a barbecue grill, turning frequently and brushing with the marinade mix. When they are well done they should be served immediately.

Arroz con Leche (Rice Pudding)

Ingredients

- 1 cup white rice
- 5 cups water
- 2 cans condensed milk
- 1 can evaporated milk
- 1 cup port wine
- 1 stick cinnamon
- Powdered cinnamon
- 1 orange rind
- 2 cloves

Preparation

1. Heat water in a large saucepan with the orange, cinnamon stick, and cloves until it boils.
2. Add rice and cook over low heat until the water is absorbed and the rice is well cooked.
3. Remove the orange rind and species, and add the 3 cans of milk.
4. Cook over low heat for some 10 minutes, stirring always with a wooden spoon to prevent sticking. The pudding must acquire a thick, creamy consistency.
5. Add the port wine and cook for 2 more minutes.
6. Remove from the heat and let cool.
7. Serve with enough cinnamon powder to cover the surface and decorate with a cinnamon stick.

Makes 8 servings.

Arroz con Mariscos (Shellfish and Rice)

Ingredients

- 1 large onion
- 2 ripe tomatoes (or canned tomatoes)
- 4 tbsp olive oil (or ordinary oil if not available)
- 2 cloves garlic
- small glass dry white wine
- Chopped parsley to taste
- 1 1/2 cups starchy rice (carolino, carnarolli...)
- 1 kilo shellfish mixture (prawns, mussels, clams, crab, whatever)
- 5 cups water
- Chili to taste
- Salt
- 3 tbsp thick cream

Preparation

1. Finely chop the onion and garlic.
2. Lightly fry with the oil until transparent.
3. Add the tomatoes, chopped.
4. Add the wine and let reduce slightly.
5. Add the rice and water.
6. Let it cook for about 10 minutes.
7. Add the shellfish and cook for a further 10 minutes.
8. Season with chili and salt to taste.

9. Add the cream.
10. Sprinkle with the parsley and serve.

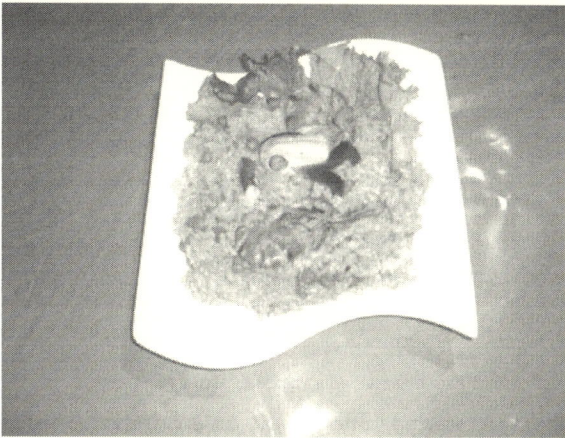

Arroz con Pollo (Chicken and Rice)

Arroz con Pollo is a traditional dish that's common throughout Latin America especially in Cuba, Panama, Peru, Puerto Rico, Costa Rica, and the Dominican Republic. Common ingredients include rice, vegetables, fresh herbs and chicken. It's a derivation of Spain's paella. Below are two recipes. The first is popular throughout the Caribbean; the second is the Peruvian recipe.

Caribbean recipe (serves four)

Ingredients

- A three to four pound chicken cut into serving pieces
- 4 cloves of fresh, minced garlic
- 1 small, finely chopped onions
- 2 cups medium or long-grain rice
- 6 cups chicken bouillon
- 1/2 oz chopped cilantro
- 8 oz canned peas (thoroughly drained)
- 8 oz diced red bell pepper
- 1 medium onion, chopped
- 1 can (15 ounce) diced tomatoes
- 6 cups chicken broth
- 1/2 tablespoon sweet paprika
- 8 saffron threads or 1 teaspoon food coloring for yellow rice
- salt and pepper to taste and olive oil

Preparation

1. Season the chicken with two pinches of salt and a pinch of pepper. Pour enough olive oil into a large skillet to just barely cover the bottom.
2. Sauté chicken in oil until brown. There are two ways to proceed from here: Either remove the chicken from the skillet or keep it there. Sauté garlic until brown. Be careful, garlic burns easily.
3. Add the onion, bell pepper, tomatoes and paprika. Sauté until the vegetables are tender. Transfer the ingredients to a large stewing pot.
4. Add the cilantro, bouillon and saffron (or food coloring). Bring to a rolling boil.
5. Add the rice and mix well. Simmer over medium heat until the rice is cooked and the liquid is absorbed. Add more broth or water if the liquid evaporates before the rice is cooked.
6. Add the chicken to the pot (if you removed it previously) and cover it with rice. Wait two to three minutes to allow the chicken to warm. Sprinkle peas on top of the rice.

Arroz con Pollo (Chicken and Rice)

Peruvian recipe (serves nine)

Ingredients

- 9 chicken drumsticks
- 9 chicken thighs
- 1 orange
- 1/2 lemon
- 1/2 lime
- Adobo (or salt)
- 1 pound chopped green pepper
- 1 pound chopped onion
- 3 garlic cloves
- 15 oz. tomato sauce
- 1 small jar chopped pimentos
- 1 1/2 cups cooking sherry
- 2 cups water
- 3 cups long-grain rice
- 1 tablespoon salt
- bay leaf
- pinch of saffron
- 1 can of peas
- olive oil

Preparation

1. Marinate the chicken for about 6 hours in the juice of 1 orange, 1/2 lemon, and 1/2 lime. Sprinkle with Adobo (or salt).

2. Brown chicken in a pan.
3. Saute onion, pepper, and garlic to make a sofrito.
4. Add tomato sauce to sofrito, cook for 5 min.
5. Add pimento, liquid from can of peas, bay leaf, salt, saffron, sherry, and water. Add chicken, cover pot, and cook for 1/2 hour on low.
6. Add rice, cook on stove on low or in oven at 350 °F until liquid is almost absorbed (about 30-45 min.).
7. Mix in peas and let them warm up before serving.

Arroz Tapado (Covered Rice)

This dish is very popular in Peru and is a favorite among children.

The minced beef preparation is very similar to picadillo which is popular throughout Latin America and the Philippines. In most other countries picadillo is served with white rice on the side.

Ingredients

- 3 cloves of garlic, minced
- 2 tablespoons of olive oil
- lemon juice
- salt
- 4 cups water
- 1 pound washed rice
- 1 onion, finely chopped
- 2 pounds of ground beef
- 2 tomatoes, finely chopped
- 1 tablespoon tomato paste
- 4 tablespoons of raisins
- 5 black olives, chopped
- 3 hard boiled eggs; two chopped, one whole
- 1 tablespoon parsley, finely minced

Preparation

1. Sauté the garlic in oil, add a few drops of lemon juice, salt and the water and bring to a boil.
2. Add rice and cook until tender. This should take 20 to 25 minutes.

3. In another pan, stir in onions and sauté.
4. Add meat, tomatoes, tomato paste, raisins, olives, egg and parsley.
5. Take an eight-ounce measuring cup and coat the inside with a little oil. Fill halfway with rice, add some meat filling and add more rice to top of cup. Invert onto a plate and carefully remove cup.
6. Cut the remaining hard-boiled egg in half and serve the two halves alongside the arroz tapado on the same plate.

Bistec a lo Pobre (Poor Man's Steak)

Ingredients

- 4 sirloin steaks cut to 1/2 inch thickness
- 4 cloves garlic, mashed
- salt, pepper, cumin and smoked paprika to taste
- 2 large onions, sliced thinly
- 4 medium Yukon Gold potatoes, peeled and sliced thinly (French fries)
- 1 packet Sazon seasoning (optional)
- 4 tbsp olive oil
- 4 extra large eggs
- 4 bananas

Preparation

1. Rub the steaks with the garlic.
2. Season with the salt, pepper, cumin and smoked paprika. Set aside.
3. Heat the oil in a large skillet or frying pan.
4. Add the onions and potatoes and sprinkle with salt, pepper and the Sazon, if using.
5. Sauté the onions and potatoes over medium to medium-high heat, until very tender, about 10 minutes.
6. Cover the pan for the first several minutes and finish it uncovered. Remove to a serving platter and keep warm.

7. In the same pan, sear the steaks on each side and cook them until they are done to your liking. Add a little more oil if needed.
8. Set the steaks aside with the potatoes and onions. Continue to keep warm.
9. Slice each banana in two pieces length-wise, and fry.
10. The eggs must be fried, sunny side up, in a nonstick pan. Leave the yolks soft and runny.
11. Lay one egg on top of each steak with the fried bananas on the side. Finally, serve all together.

Causa

Causa is one of the most popular dishes all along Peru's coast. Besides being delicious, the traditional causa is fairly economic and easy to prepare, making it accessible to the rich and the poor, great chefs and terrible cooks. Moreover, it's a versatile dish that allows for many variations, both in the purée and in the fillings.

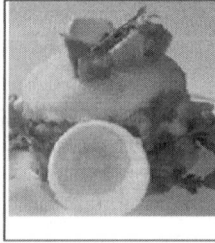

The following is the classic recipe, a potatoes and ají amarillo mash filled with tuna and avocado.

Ingredients

- 1kg potatoes (yellow, if available)
- 4 tbsp ají amarillo paste
- ½ cup vegetable oil (olive oil not recommended)
- Juice 1 key lime
- 1 can of tuna-fish packed in oil
- ½ onion, finely chopped
- 1 cup mayonnaise
- 1 avocado
- Salt

Preparation

1. Boil the potatoes in salted water.
2. Peel and mash while still hot (enough to handle).

3. Let cool and mix thoroughly with the ají amarillo paste, vegetable oil, and lime juice.
4. Salt to taste.
5. Mix the tuna with the chopped onions and mayonnaise.
6. Place a layer of the potato mash on a serving dish, and spread with a thin film of mayonnaise.
7. Cut the avocado in slices and lay on the first layer of potato mash.
8. Spread a second layer of potato mash, and cover with the tuna mayonnaise.
9. Cover with a last layer of potatoes, and decorated with slices of hard boiled eggs and black olives.

Tip: try variations of the filling using (instead of tuna) crab-meat, shrimp, octopus in olive, or (for vegetarians) plain tomato slices.

Ají Amarillo Paste

Using 1lb (½ kg) fresh ají Amarillo and 2 tbsp. of vegetable oil, place ají in a saucepan with water and boil (for some 5 minutes after water boils). Change water and repeat procedure twice; cut, seed and devein ajíes. You can peel some ajíes to reduce spiciness; and blend with the oil until you get a creamy paste.

As an alternative to fresh ají amarillo, you can use dried chilli-peppers (known as dried ají mirasol), which are easier to find outside of Peru. The procedure is similar as with the fresh ajíes, just add some water when blending until you get the creamy paste.

Causa Rellena con Cangrejo (Stuffed with Crab)

A "causa" is a dish of layered ingredients which is served cold as a light entrée or first course on warm days, making it an ideal dish for summer entertaining.

Ingredients - Relish

- 1/2 large red onion, finely chopped
- 1/2 cup white vinegar
- 1 (4-ounce) can sliced jalapeño peppers, with their juice
- 1/3 bunch cilantro, leaves and stems, finely chopped
- salt and pepper to taste
- 1 (8-ounce) jar roasted yellow peppers, strained and finely chopped
- Juice of 1/2 a lime

Ingredients - Causa Layers

- 2 pounds Yukon potatoes
- Salt and pepper to taste
- Juice of 2 limes
- 1/4 cup canola or corn oil
- 1 (16-ounce) can lump crab meat, drained
- 1/4 cup mayonnaise
- 2 avocados, sliced
- 6 large romaine lettuce leaves, sliced

Preparation

1. Grease a 12-inch rectangular bread mold with a bit of oil, then line it with 2 large pieces of plastic wrap, making sure they overlap so all the bottom and sides of the mold are covered and there is enough wrap on the sides of the mold with which to fold over and tightly cover the causa once it has been assembled. Set aside.

2. For the relish, put onions and vinegar into a medium bowl, cover and set aside for 45 minutes. Meanwhile, place the jalapeños and their juice into a blender and blend until smooth. Strain the mixture through a fine sieve, separating the juice from pulp left over. Save the juice and pulp separately in small bowls. Strain the onions, discarding the vinegar and return to the bowl. Add cilantro, salt and pepper, 1/2 cup of the yellow peppers, lime juice and 1 tablespoon of the reserved jalapeño pulp. Cover and set relish aside. (Save the remaining jalapeño pulp and juice for later use in the causa.)

3. For the causa, place potatoes in a large pot and cover by 2 inches with cold water. Add 2 tablespoons salt and bring to a boil. Cook for about 25 minutes, until potatoes are tender when pierced with a knife. Drain and let potatoes cool until you can handle them safely. Peel potatoes and press them through a potato ricer or the fine side of a

cheese grater, making sure no lumps remain. Transfer potatoes to a large bowl and add the juice of 1 lime, oil and 1/4 cup of the reserved jalapeño juice. Mix with a potato masher, adding salt and pepper to taste. Place in the refrigerator until cooled.

4. Meanwhile, mix crab meat with mayonnaise and juice from 1/2 a lime. Season with salt and pepper, cover and refrigerate. Put avocados, remaining juice from 1/2 a lime, salt and pepper into a bowl and toss gently to combine.

5. Use a large spoon to spread one-third of the potato mixture into a layer at the bottom of the bread mold. Arrange half of the avocado slices in the mold for the next layer, making sure all corners and sides of the mold are covered. Transfer about 6 dollops of the crab meat mixture to a small bowl, cover and refrigerate for later use. Spread half of the remaining crab meat mixture into the mold to make the next layer. Press down firmly with the back of a spoon. Repeat with one more layer each of the potato mixture, avocados and crab, then finish with a layer of potato mixture on top. Fold the plastic wrap over the top of the mold to cover completely. Press down slightly along the top of the mold, then refrigerate for at least 1 hour.

6. To serve, carefully uncover the plastic wrap and unmold the causa over a serving plate. Spread some of the reserved relish over the top of the causa. Arrange lettuce leaves on 6 serving plates. Cut the causa carefully into six slices and place one slice on top of the lettuce on each serving plate. Add more of the relish and a dollop of the reserved crab meat mix on top of each slice. Serve immediately.

Causa Rellena con Pollo (Stuffed with Chicken)

Ingredients

- 10 medium potatoes (yellow, new, or red are a good choice)
- 1 pound of shredded boiled chicken meat
- 100 g mayonnaise
- 25 g butter
- 2 cloves garlic
- salt and pepper
- lettuce
- 3 hard boiled eggs
- black olives

Preparation

1. Cook and peel potatoes and allow to cool, then mash.
2. In a bowl combine the chicken, mayonnaise, onion, salt and pepper.
3. Line a deep dish with plastic wrap, or place a molding cylinder on a plate.
4. Add the mashed potatoes to form a bed about 1 cm tall at the bottom.
5. Add a second layer of 1 cm of the chicken mixture evenly over the potato.
6. Top the chicken mixture with a final layer of potato, forming a sandwich of chicken inside two layers of potato.
7. De-mold or remove the cylinder.

8. Garnish with lettuce and mayonnaise.
9. Cut the hard boiled eggs in discs and place on top. Add black olives, if desired.
10. This dish can be served slightly cold.

Variations

Mashed potatoes can be prepared with a mix of olive oil and butter and adding one tablespoon of lemon juice. You can compensate lemon with salt. (Don't add milk)

You can as well replace chicken with a can of tuna mixed with mayonnaise and fine chopped onion. Serve this variation fresh only.

Ceviche de Pescado (Fish)

Ceviche is a traditional Peruvian dish. In its classic form, it is composed of chunks of raw fish, lime juice, chopped onion, and minced ají limo or rocoto, both types of chiles.

Ingredients

- 2 pounds of white fish (mahi mahi is an excellent choice)
- juice from about 6 large limes
- 2 red peppers, diced
- 2 finely diced jalapeño peppers (to your preference)
- salt and pepper to taste
- 1 large onion, sliced into half-rings
- bunch of finely chopped cilantro
- Sides:
  - 2 lettuce leaves per plate
  - 12 to 16 corn cobs cut into 2 inch pieces, cooked as usual
  - 3 or 4 sweet potatoes, boiled and peeled

Preparation

1. Wash and de-bone the fish and cut them into ½ inch by ½ inch chunks.
2. Season the fish with salt, pepper, red pepper and jalapeño. Marinate the fish for 1 hour to "cold cook". You should have enough lime juice to completely cover the fish.

3. Add onion. Mix gently. Marinate for 1 more hour.
4. Serve on a bed of lettuce and add two pieces of corn-on-the-cob and a portion of sweet potato.

Ceviche can be eaten as an entrée as well. In this case, this will be enough for about two people.

More traditional recipes call for much less marinating. In fact, some will marinate it for as little as 10 minutes total (basically just the time it takes to get the sides ready). If marinating for a small amount of time be aware that the acidity of the lime is the only thing that "cooks" the fish.

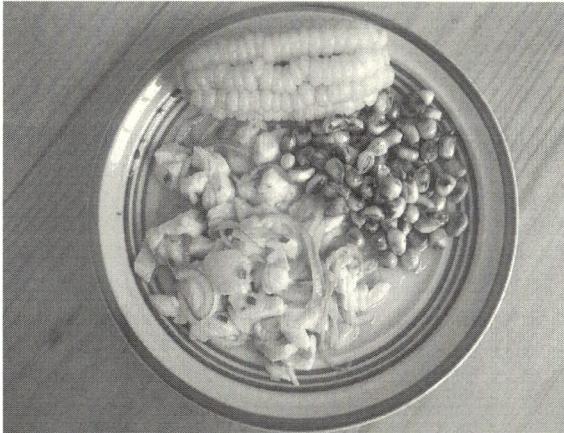

Ceviche de Camarones y Pescado (Shrimp and Fish)

Ingredients

- 1 pound Shrimp (16/20 per pound), peeled and cleaned
- 2 pounds meaty white fish, boned, and cut into large dice
- 1 red Onion, minced
- 1 piece Ginger, peeled, minced
- 1 clove Garlic, minced
- 1/4 Habañero or Scotch bonnet Pepper, minced (no seeds or ribs)
- 1 Celery rib, minced
- Salt and Black Pepper
- 5 Lemons, juiced
- 5 Limes, juiced
- 1 bunch Cilantro, chopped
- 2 ears of Corn, grilled with husk on

Preparation

1. Boil salted water. Have ice water ready on the side. Poach shrimp for just 30 seconds and cool in ice water and drain.
2. Combine with fish and toss with onion, ginger, garlic, hot pepper, celery, salt, and black pepper. Allow to cool in the refrigerator at least 30 minutes and up to 2 hours.

3. Add lemon and lime juices and refrigerate 1 additional hour. Finish with cilantro and corn, check seasoning.

Yield: 8 to 12 servings

Chicha Morada (Purple Corn Drink)

Chica Morada is a powerful antioxidant drink made from purple corn. The recipe makes 24 quarts but could be easily reduced by half or three-quarters.

Ingredients

- 8 bags (15 ounces each) purple corn
- 8 green apples
- 2 pineapples (peeled and cored)
- 2 quince
- 10 cinnamon sticks
- 20 whole cloves
- 15 cups sugar, or to taste
- 1 quart freshly squeezed key lime juice, or to taste

Preparation

1. Wash, peel and cut fruit into pieces. Reserve the skins.
2. Cut the corn kernels from the cob.
3. Combine the fruit, fruit skins, corn kernels and spices in a large pot with enough water to cover. Cook for approximately one hour, or until the water takes on a deep purple color and is infused with flavors.
4. Strain and let the liquid cool. Add sugar and lime juice to taste.

Chicharrón de Cerdo (Fried Pork)

Pork chicharron is a very popular dish in all regions of Peru. Usually, it's served with onion sauce. This recipe is easy and is for 8 to 10 people.

Ingredients - Chicarron

- 2 kg (4 1/2 lb) of pork in pieces
- Sweet potatoes
- Onion sauce
- Water
- Salt
- Pepper
- Cumin
- Mint
- Pisco (optional)
- Vinegar

Ingredients – Onion Sauce

- 1 medium onion
- 1 tablespoon of vegetable oil
- 1 fresh yellow pepper, chopped and cleaned (without seeds)
- 1/2 teaspoon of lime juice.
- Salt
- Pepper
- 1/2 tablespoon of chopped cilantro.

Preparation

1. Marinade the pork with salt, pepper, cumin, mint and a little of vinegar for 15 to 20 minutes.
2. Put the pork in a pot and cover the meat with water.
3. Put the top on the pot and boil on a low flame until the water gets evaporated. Open the pot and fry in its own fat until it gets browned and soft.
4. Cook the sweet potatoes and cut in thin slices. Fry them.
5. Prepare the onion sauce by cutting the onion in stripes, wash it in water and mix it with the rest of ingredients.
6. Serve the pork chicharron with sweet potato slices and onion sauce.

Choros a la Chalaca (Mussels Peruvian Style)

Ingredients

- 12 mussels tightly closed
- 2 medium size onions, finely chopped
- Juice of 3 key limes
- 1 tablespoon ají amarillo fresco / fresh yellow aji (chili), blended
- ½ rocoto / red hot pepper, rinsed, seeded and deveined, finely chopped
- 1 ½ tablespoon parsley, finely chopped
- ¾ cups corn kernels, cooked
- ½ tomato, peeled, seeded and cut in small cubes
- 1 tablespoon oil
- Salt and pepper
- 1 key lime, cut in wedges to serve

Preparation

1. Rinse mussels thoroughly and scrub under running water. Discard any mussels that are not tightly closed.
2. Cook mussels in boiling water and remove from pan as soon as they open, to prevent overcooking them. Discard mussels that do not open. Cool.
3. Open mussels with a knife and place half on a serving dish.

4. Combine in a medium size bowl, onion, red hot pepper, tomato, parsley, corn, ají, oil, key lime juice, salt and pepper. Let mixture stand for 15 minutes.
5. Place approximately 1 ½ tablespoon of this mixture over each mussel.
6. Serve with lime wedges.

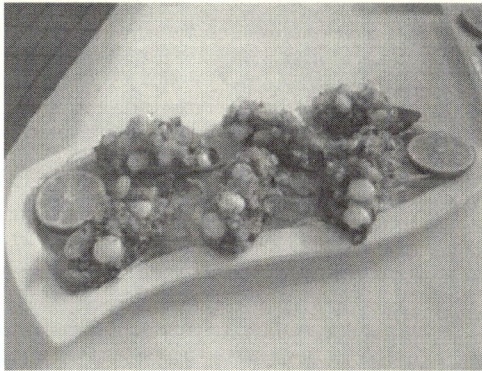

Chupe de Camarones (Shrimp Soup)

Ingredients

- 2 bags of shrimp
- 3 onions
- 1 block of "Queso Fresco"
- 1 can evaporated milk
- 1 butternut squash
- 3 carrots
- 1 can or bag of peas
- Aji colorado
- Oregano
- 1/2 cup of rice
- one piece of fried fish
- 2 cans chicken broth
- 1 corn-on-the-cob per person
- Eggs- more or less one egg per person

Preparation

1. Fry the onions until they are golden with a teaspoon of aji colorado (panca)
2. Separately boil the squash and the carrots until they are soft
3. Separately fry the fish with salt and pepper
4. Over the fried onions put the 2 cans of broth, the squash (without skin) and the carrots (smashed)
5. Add the cheese in squares, the rice and peas.

6. Add the eggs one at a time, mixing so that they do not stay whole.
7. Boil all of the above under high heat.
8. Add salt to taste.
9. Add the corn.
10. 10 minutes before serving, add the cooked shrimp (peeled).
11. Add oregano in little leaves.
12. 5 minutes before serving, add the can of milk and mix everything.

Ensalada de Pallares (Lima Bean Salad)

Ingredients

- 1 lb (500g) pallares (large lima beans)
- water
- salt
- 1 cup olive oil
- 2-3 teaspoons white vinegar
- 1 spoonful Dijon mustard
- pepper
- 1 red onion, finely diced
- 2 tomatoes
- a few sprigs of parsley

Preparation

1. Soak one pound of pallares (large lima beans) overnight or at least 6 hours. Change water two or three times.
2. Boil the beans (without salt) with enough water to cover them. Use high heat until water reaches boiling point. Skim and reduce your fire. Simmer for about 1 hour. No exact timing is possible, since cooking time depends on the dryness of the beans.
3. When the beans are plump and tender, take them off the heat and drain. You might save the boiling liquid to make leftovers into a soup.

4. Season the beans lightly with salt (kosher works great) and, while the beans cool down, prepare your vinaigrette.
5. Mix one cup of olive oil, two or three spoonfuls of white vinegar, one spoonful of Dijon mustard, salt and pepper to taste, one finely diced small red onion, and two diced seeded tomatoes.
6. About half to one hour later, once the beans are at room temperature, check the seasoning of the vinaigrette. It should taste a bit stronger than expected.
7. Carefully mix the vinaigrette with the beans. Finely cut a few sprigs of parsley and mix again.
8. Reserve some more parsley for decoration.

Estofado de Pollo (Chicken Stew)

Ingredients

- One medium chicken in quarters
- 1/3 cup of oil
- 1 1/2 cups chopped onions
- 1 garlic clove - grounded
- 1 small can tomato paste (90 grams)
- 3/4 cups Sauterne wine
- 1/2 cup peas
- 1/2 cup chopped carrots
- 6 medium sized potatoes (boiled)

Preparation

1. In a medium sized pan brown the chicken in the oil, then separate
2. In the same pan and oil, fry onions and garlic. Add the tomato paste, wine, salt, pepper, peas and carrots. Mix well.
3. Place chicken over everything. Cover and cook in low heat for 15 minutes or until the chicken is cooked. Add the potatoes
4. Serve with rice

Lomo Saltado (Jumping Beef)

Lomo Saltado is a dish of marinated steak, vegetables and French fried potatoes, usually served over white rice. It is one of the most popular recipes in Peru and is often found on the menu at many smaller restaurants at a very reasonable price.

Ingredients

- 3pounds (900g) of beef tenderloin or other tender steak
- ¼ cup red wine, e.g. Burgundy
- 2 tablespoons of crushed garlic
- 2 medium onions cut in strips
- 4 tomatoes, cut in strips
- 1 yellow Peruvian Chili Pepper (aji) cut into thin strips
- 1 tablespoon of vinegar
- 2 tablespoons of soy sauce
- vegetable oil for frying
- salt and pepper
- culantro (or substitute with cilantro)
- 3 pounds of French fried potatoes

Preparation

1. Cut the meat into thin strips and marinate them in the wine for 1 hour.
2. Use a wok to cook garlic in oil over medium heat and add the meat. Save the juice.
3. Add the soy sauce while stirring the meat in the wok.

4. Add the tomatoes, salt and pepper.
5. Add the onions, aji strips, cilantro and vinegar. Combine the juice from the meat. Cook a few minutes.
6. Add French fries to the other ingredients.
7. Serve the dish with white rice.

Ocopa (Peruvian Green Sauce)

Ocopa is a Peruvian green sauce commonly served over potatoes. It originates from the city of Arequipa.   A variation is to serve the green sauce with shrimp (Ocopa de Camarones).

Ingredients

- 8 crushed ajies (jalapenos) will work I guess
- 2 garlic cloves
- 3 crakers saltines or unsalted
- 1 lb of ricotta cheese or feta cheese
- 1 tbp of oil
- 1/2 tbs of cilantro
- 1/2 tbs of huacatay (optional) is a oeruvian herb
- 3/4 cup of condesed milk
- 3 tbp of roasted peanuts
- Bolied potatoes
- hard boiled eggs
- lettuce leaves

Preparation

1. Roast the ajies (jalapenos), clean them up, take all the inside, and wash them in water.
2. Cover them in water and take put them on the stove top, as soon it starts boiling, take from the heat, and change water with fresh water and repeat the operation three times in total.

3. Heat the oil just a little bit, garlic, peanuts, crackers, cheese in the blender and start mixing and add the oil little by little. You should have a semi thick cream.
4. In a plate put the lettuce leaves first, on top the boiled potatoes cut in half, cover with the sauce and decorate with slices of hard-boiled egg on top

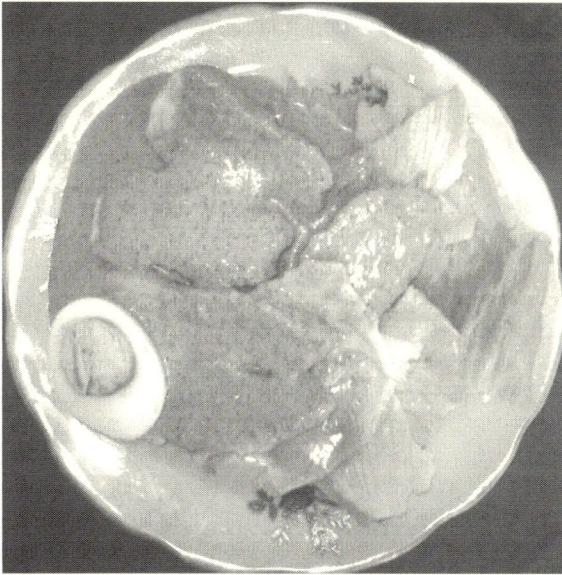

Ocopa de Camarones (Shrimp)

Ingredients

- 7 oz ¼ lb (200 g) ají mirasol / sundried yellow aji (chili)
- garlic clove
- ½ medium-size onion, coarsely cut
- 12 nuts
- 10 graham crackers
- Oil (necessary quantity)
- 2.2 lb (1 k) shrimp
- ¾ cup olive oil
- ½ key lime
- Salt
- Pepper
- 1 ½ cup boiled water

Preparation

1. Cut, seed and devein aji, using gloves. Wash thoroughly with water, rubbing insides one against the other.
2. Place aji, onion and garlic on baking sheet and take to oven 350° F (175° C) until golden.
3. Shell and devein shrimp. Set tails aside.
4. Fry shrimp heads, claws and shells in ½ cup olive oil. Liquefy this in blender with 1 ½ cup boiled water. Strain. Save liquid.

5. Remove aji from baking sheet and place in bowl. Cover with water just boiled for 4 or 5 hours. This process will take hotness from aji. Discard water.

6. Blend or process aji, onion, garlic, nuts, and graham crackers with the reserved liquid from shrim. While blending, start pouring oil until mixture resembles a creamy sauce. Season with salt and pepper.

7. Fry shrimp tails in ½ cup olive oil. Add few drops of key lime, salt and pepper and continue frying until shrimp turn pink in color.

8. Serve ocopa sauce over slices of boiled potatoes, with hardboiled eggs, lettuce and olives.

9. Garnish with shrimp tails.

Papas a la Huancaína (Potatoes)

Ingredients

- 10 medium potatoes (new or red are a good choice)
- 1 pound of cheese (Romano, Mexican or feta work well)
- 4 aji amarillo, seeded and deveined (Peruvian yellow chili peppers)
- 1 cup evaporated milk
- ½ cup vegetable oil
- 2 cloves garlic
- 8 saltine crackers
- 1 tablespoon prepared mustard
- salt and pepper
- 3 hard boiled eggs
- lettuce and black olives

Preparation

1. Peel and boil potatoes as you normally would. Drain water, and allow them to cool.
2. In a blender, mix the cheese, peppers, milk, oil, garlic, crackers, mustard, salt and pepper. The sauce should be fairly thick; add more crackers if not, or add milk if too thick.
3. Lay a bed of lettuce in a serving dish and place the potatoes on top. Cover with the sauce. Cut the hard boiled eggs in half and place on top of the potatoes. Add black olives if desired.

4. This dish can be served slightly cold.

Some recipes suggest the use of Huacatay, but this is a confusion. Huacatay is a key ingredient of Ocopa, another Peruvian sauce.

Papa Rellena (Stuffed Potato)

Papa rellena is a delicious comfort food, similar to mashed potato pancakes, but with a surprise ground beef center. In fact, this is an excellent recipe for using up leftover mashed potatoes. To make papas rellenas, you first prepare some seasoned ground beef filling, similar to an empanada filling. Then you mold some mashed potatoes around a center of ground beef, and you form the whole thing into an oblong shape - basically you make it look like a potato! Then you fry it in oil until it is golden brown and crispy. Kids love this meal, especially with ketchup.

Ingredients

- 1/2 cup raisins
- 3 pounds yellow potatoes
- 1/2 cup chopped onion
- 2 cloves garlic, minced
- 1 tablespoon minced aji pepper, or jalapeno
- 1 teaspoon cumin
- 1/2 teaspoon paprika
- 1 pound ground beef
- 1 cup beef broth
- 1 egg
- Flour for dusting
- Salt and pepper to taste

Preparation

1. Place the raisins in a small bowl and pour 1 cup boiling water over them. Let them soak for 10 minutes.
2. Bring a large pot of salted water to a boil. Peel the potatoes and place them in the pot.

Cook the potatoes until they are tender when pierced with a fork.

3. While the potatoes are cooking, cook the onions, garlic, and peppers in the vegetable oil until soft and fragrant.
4. Add the cumin and paprika and cook 2 minutes more, stirring. Add the ground beef and cook until browned.
5. Drain the raisins and add them to the ground beef. Add the beef broth and simmer for 10 to 15 minutes more, until most of the liquid is gone.
6. Season mixture with salt and pepper to taste. Remove from heat and let cool.
7. When the potatoes are cooked, drain them in a colander. Mash the potatoes thoroughly, or pass them through a potato ricer. Season the mashed potatoes with salt and pepper to taste. Chill the potatoes for several hours, or overnight.
8. Once the potatoes are very cold, stir the egg into the mashed potatoes until well mixed.

Pescado a la Chorrillana (Fish)

Chorrillos is a district in the south of Lima, a former resort about the middle of the 19th century. It's popular for its beaches and seafood-based dishes, one of which is the Chorrillos-style fish. It contains (as well as fish), onions, garlic, tomatoes, yellow chili/pepper and cilantro. It's simple and tasty! This recipe is for 6 people.

Ingredients

- 6 fillets of fish
- Lime juice
- Flour
- 1/2 cup of vegetable oil
- 2 medium onions, cut in thick slices
- 2 cloves of garlic, finely chopped
- 2 tomatoes, peeled, without seeds and cut in pieces
- Yellow chili/pepper, ground, to one's taste
- 1 yellow chili/pepper, clean, without seeds and cut in strips
- 1 tablespoon of chopped cilantro
- Salt and pepper

Preparation

1. Season the fillets, flour and fry them in hot vegetable oil. Keep back covered in a bowl (you don't want they get cooled down!).
2. Heat vegetable oil and fry the onion. Add the garlic. Cook until the onion get light. Add the ground chili/pepper, chili/pepper strips, tomato and cilantro. Season.
3. Put over this mix the fillets and cook 5 minutes on a low flame. Pour the lime juice.

4. Serve with rice and cooked potatoes.

Pisco Sour

The famous Pisco sour, invented in Peru around 1900, is made with Pisco (a very classy grape brandy from the Andean country) and has a bit of bite of secret ingredients to create the balance in this creamy, frothy, limey drink.

Ingredients

- 7 ½ oz (or 3 parts) Peruvian Pisco
- 2 ½ oz (1 part) key lime juice
- 2 ½ oz (1 part) sugar syrup
- 1 egg white
- Angostura bitter

Preparation

1. Pour the Pisco, key lime juice and syrup on a jar blender with enough ice to double the volume.
2. Blend on high. Add one egg white and blend again.
3. Serve. Pour a drop of Angostura bitter on each glass.

Tip: to make the sugar syrup just put ½ cup of sugar in a pot with 3 tbs. of water, bring to a slow boil (always stirring), and cook until all the sugar has dissolved. Let the syrup cool before mixing with the Pisco and lime juice.

Here is another variation of the Pisco sour:

Ingredients

- 3 cups of Pisco
- 1 ½ cup of sugar
- 2 cups of lemon juice
- 1 egg's white
- Ice flakes
- Add drops of Amargo Angostura

Preparation

1. Prepare the pisco sour in a blender. Place the egg white and blend for a few seconds.
2. Add the ice only until it reaches the middle of glass (this is the secret to get that the drink has a very heavy texture) move it and add all the ingredients but the Angostura.
3. Mix it all.

It might be necessary to add some ice water and rectify the quality of a great Pisco sour.

Pulpo al Olivo (Octopus in Olive Sauce)

Ingredients

- 1 egg
- 1 cup olive oil
- 2 tsp key lime juice
- 10 black olives, pitted
- 2lbs 5 oz (1.2kg) octopus
- 1 tbs minced parsley
- Salt

Preparation

1. Boil octopus (completely covered with water) for about 45 minutes, until soft.

2. Remove the skin with a knife, and refrigerate (the octopus is much easier to slice when cold).
3. Blend the egg, salt, lime juice (steel blade recommended). While blending, pour slowly and steadily the olive oil to obtain a thick mayonnaise. Set aside half of the mayonnaise, leaving the other half in the blender.
4. Add the olives and blend until you get a creamy pure. Mix it with the mayonnaise until getting a uniform mixture.
5. Lay the octopus slices on a plate (single layer) and cover with the olive sauce. Garnish with freshly minced parsley and a trickle of olive oil.

Makes 6 servings

Rocoto Relleno (Stuffed Hot Peppers)

Hot, delicious and very unique. One of the most well known rocoto dishes in Peru is the rocoto relleno. This is a traditional entree from the Andean city of Arequipa, made with rocoto (chili pepper). Besides the meat, it can be stuffed with many another ingredients. As for the ideal stuffing, this beef mix contains beef, pork, onion, garlic, margarine (or butter), cream, pecans and it will be a heavenly meal.

Ingredients

- 7 rocotos with a wide base
- 3/4 cup of red vinegar
- 200 g (1/2 lb) of ground beef
- 100 g (1/4 lb) of ground pork
- 3 tablespoons of olive oil
- 3 tablespoons of tomato sauce
- 1/2 glass of dry white wine
- 2 tablespoons of cream

- 1/4 cup of ground pecans
- 1/2 cup of beef stock
- 1 tablespoon of aji panca paste
- 6 small potatoes, cooked and peeled
- 1 red onion, chopped
- 2 cloves of garlic, ground
- 1/4 cup or margarine or butter
- 1/2 tablespoon of flour
- 3/4 cup of mozzarella cheese
- 1/2 cup of grated parmesan cheese
- 2 tablespoons of chopped garlic

Preparation

1. The Rocotos (Chili Pepper): In the first place, cut the upper part of 7 rocotos as a lid. It's extremely important to take out all the seeds and to clean it.
2. Cook in water with salt and vinegar. Repeat this process four times.
3. Prepare the stuffing: Make a seasoning in a frying pan with the margarine, the ground garlic and onion. Once you do this, add the aji panca paste.
4. Then, you must season the meats with salt and pepper and add them to the seasoning. Mix well.
5. Chop the remaining rocoto (in very small pieces) and add it with the pecans and the flour. Mix again.
6. Wait some moments and add the stock and cream.
7. Mix and take out from the flame.

8. Using hot oil, fry the chopped garlic in olive oil, add the tomato sauce and the wine. Let it cook for 5 minutes.
9. Now, stuff the rocotos with the meat mix. It's mandatory to be gentle in order to keep the rocotos intact.
10. Spread tomato sauce on a tray and place the stuffed rocotos and the potatoes. Cover them with parmesan and mozzarella cheese.
11. You are almost done! Bake to 350º F (150º C) until the cheeses get melt.
12. Serve immediately with white baked potatoes and salad.

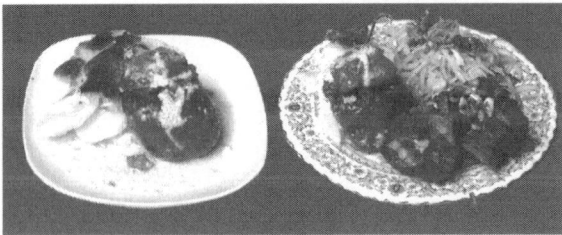

Seco de Cordero (Lamb Stew)

Seco de cordero is a delicious Peruvian lamb stew. Seasoned with aji peppers, cumin, and lots of cilantro, the lamb is braised in beer until it's tender and flavorful. Yellow potatoes cook at the same time and soak up all the great flavor. This recipe calls for one aji amarillo pepper, which gives the dish a traditional kick of spiciness, but you can adjust the amount of hot pepper to your preference. Serve seco de cordero over South American-style rice.

Ingredients

- 2 pounds lamb meat (shoulder or leg)
- 1/2 cup vinegar
- 1 teaspoon cumin
- 3 cloves garlic, minced
- 1/4 cup vegetable oil
- 1 large red onion, chopped fine
- 1 aji pepper (or other hot chile pepper), chopped fine
- 4 tablespoons vegetable oil
- 1 bunch of cilantro
- 1 bottle of beer
- 1-2 cups chicken or beef stock
- 5-6 medium yellow potatoes

Preparation

1. Cut the meat into approximate 2 inch cubes.

2. Mix the vinegar with the garlic, cumin, 1/4 cup vegetable oil, and some salt and black pepper, and pour over the meat. Let meat marinate at room temperature for 30 minutes to an hour.

3. Purée the cilantro (stems removed) with some water in a blender or food processor until you get a smooth paste.

4. Heat 3-4 tablespoons oil in a large pot or skillet on high heat. Working in 2 batches, brown the meat on all sides. Remove meat to a plate.

5. Lower the heat and add the onion and aji pepper to the same skillet with the leftover marinade. Cook until soft and fragrant, about 5 minutes.

6. Add the meat back to the skillet, along with the beer, the cilantro, and 1 cup of the chicken stock. Cover and cook over low heat until the meat is tender, about an hour.

7. Peel and quarter the potatoes, and add them to the stew. Continue to cook over low heat until potatoes are tender, about 30 minutes more, adding more chicken broth if necessary.

8. Serve warm over rice.

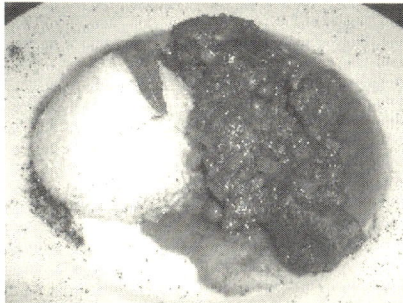

Suspiro a la Limeña (Lima-Style Sigh)

The Suspiro is a traditional Peruvian dessert from the coastal cities. The preparation is easy and very simple, yet the flavor is outstanding.

Ingredients

- 1 (14 ounce) can sweetened condensed milk
- 1 (12 fluid ounce) can evaporated milk
- 1 tablespoon vanilla extract
- 2 beaten egg yolks
- 2 beaten egg white
- 1 cup confectioners' sugar
- 1/4 teaspoon ground cinnamon (optional)

Preparation

1. Whisk together the sweetened condensed milk, evaporated milk, vanilla, and egg yolks in a saucepan.
2. Place over medium-low heat and gently cook until the mixture thickens, stirring constantly with a wooden spoon, about 30 minutes.
3. Pour into a heatproof serving dish and set aside.
4. Whip the egg whites with confectioners' sugar to stiff peaks.
5. Spread meringue on top of milk mixture.
6. Refrigerate until cold, for 3 hours.
7. Finally, sprinkle with cinnamon before serving.

Tacu-Tacu

Originally, tacu-tacu was prepared with leftover seasoned beans and rice, which resulted in a very economical and nutritious dish. Today it's usually prepared on-the-moment, and served with fried eggs and bananas. It can also be served with fried beef or seafood.

Ingredients

- 2 cups canary beans, left to soak overnight
- 1 lb (½ kg) pork fat or bacon, diced
- 1 cups of cooked rice
- 2 tbsp vegetable oil
- 1 large onion, finely chopped
- 3 garlic cloves, finely chopped
- ½ cup ají amarillo paste
- Salt and pepper

Preparation

1. Drain and cook beans in unsalted water together with pork fat until soft (about 90 minutes). Set aside and let cool. Mash beans with a spoon or fork, just enough to obtain a rough purée.
2. In a large skillet, sauté in hot oil the garlic and onions until the latter acquire a golden color. Add the ají amarillo and cook for an additional couple of minutes Add the beans and rice, stirring and turning over with a wooden spoon to mix well. Salt and pepper to taste.

3. Serve with anything you like: fried eggs, fried
    banana, fried tenderloin beef, or seafood.

Tip: to enhance the taste, pour some olive oil on the
tacu-tacu. Lima beans may be substituted for canary
beans.

Tiradito (new cousin of Ceviche)

Tiradito, the new cousin of ceviche, has only become well-known in the last 20 years or so. Its origins can be found in the approach of Japanese immigrants to eating raw fish, though some suggest it is closer to Italian carpaccio, popularized earlier in the 20th century by Genovese immigrants.

Two are the main differences between them: the cut and onions. While ceviche is cut in bite-size cubes and comprises a generous amount of onions, tiradito is sliced in fine, long pieces and carries no onions.

Ingredients

- 600g of white fish (sea bass, flounder, grouper, sole, etc).
- Juice of 15 key limes
- 1 ají limo seeded, deveined, and finely diced
- 4 tbsp ají amarillo paste
- 1 tbsp fresh ginger, chopped
- 1 tbsp freshly chopped cilantro
- Salt and pepper

Preparation

1. Make a dressing with the lime juice, ají limo, ají amarillo paste, ginger, salt, and pepper. Set aside (preferably in the fridge).
2. Slice the fish into fine, sashimi-like pieces (stripes about 6cm long, 2.5cm wide, and 1,5cm thick). Place in a cold serving dish, the pieces on a single layer. Sprinkle with salt and pepper.
3. Cover with the dressing and serve immediately.

As with ceviche, tiradito can be garnished with sweet potatoes and boiled corn grains.

Tortillas de Camarones (Shrimp Tortillas)

Ingredients

- 1/2 pound small shrimp, peeled
- 1 1/2 cups chickpea or regular flour
- 1 tablespoon chopped fresh flat-leaf parsley
- 3 scallions, white part and a little of the tender green tops, finely chopped
- 1/2 teaspoon sweet pimenton
- Salt
- Olive oil for deep-frying

Preparation

1. In a saucepan, combine the shrimp with water to cover and bring to a boil over high heat
2. As soon as the water starts to boil, quickly lift out the shrimp with a slotted spoon and set aside. Scoop out 1 cup of the cooking water and let cool. Discard the remaining water. When the shrimp are cool, cover and refrigerate until needed.
3. To make the batter, combine the flour, parsley, scallions and pimentón in a bowl or a food processor. Add a pinch of salt and the cooled cooking water. Mix or process well until you obtain a texture slightly thicker than a pancake batter. Cover and refrigerate for 1 hour.

4. Remove the shrimp from the refrigerator and mince finely. The pieces should be the size of coffee grounds. Remove the batter from the refrigerator, add the shrimp, and mix well.

5. Pour the olive oil to a depth of about 1 inch into a heavy sauté pan and heat over high heat until it is almost smoking. Add 1 tablespoon of the batter to the oil for each fritter and, using the back of the spoon, immediately flatten the batter into a round 3 1/2 inches in diameter. Do not crowd the pan.

6. Fry, turning once, for about 1 minute on each side, or until the fritters are golden and very crisp with what Spanish cooks call puntillas, or lacelike formations, on the borders.

7. Using a slotted spoon, lift out the fritters, holding them briefly over the pan to allow the excess oil to drain, and transfer to an ovenproof platter lined with paper towels to drain further.

8. Keep the fritters warm in a low oven. Fry the rest of the batter in the same way, always making sure the oil is very hot before frying more fritters.

9. When all the fritters are fried, arrange them on a platter and serve immediately.

About the Author

Philip Martin McCaulay is an Actuary with a degree in Mathematics who has published books on pensions, investments, finance, real estate, card games, and massage therapy. He has traveled to seventeen different countries and found the Peruvian cuisine to be his favorite in the entire world.

His personal favorite Peruvian dishes are Lomo Saltado, Crab Causa, Bistec a lo Pobre, Papa Rellena, Seco de Cordero, Tacu-Tacu, Alfajores, and Chica Morada.

Reference List

Cooking in Peru, available at http://yanuq.com/.

Cuisine of Peru, available at
http://commons.wikimedia.org/wiki/Category:Cuisine_of_Peru

Peruvian Cuisine Blogspot, *Peruvian Cuisine*, available at
http://peruvian-cuisine.blogspot.com/.

Peru Recipes, available at http://www.justperu.org/.

Peru Recipes, available at http://www.peru-recipes.com/.

Peruvian Recipes, available at
http://recipes.peruanista.com/.

Recipes, available at http://www.epicurean.com/.

Recipes, available at http://www.grouprecipes.com/.

Recipes, available at
http://www.wholefoodsmarket.com/.

South American Food, available at
http://southamericanfood.about.com/.

Spain Recipes, available at http://www.spain-recipes.com/.

The Peru Guide, *Peruvian Cuisine Recipes*, available at
http://www.theperuguide.com/gastronomy/peruvian_cuisine_recipes.html.

Wikibooks, *Cookbook: Cuisine of Peru*, available at
http://en.wikibooks.org/wiki/Cookbook:Cuisine_of_Peru.

Wikipedia, *Food of Peru*, available at
http://en.wikipedia.org/wiki/Food_of_Peru.

966023

Printed in Great Britain by
Amazon.co.uk, Ltd.,
Marston Gate.